D0882721

Highlife
for
Caliban

Lemuel Johnson

ardis

Lemuel Johnson
Highlife for Caliban

Ardis New Poets in America Series

ISBN 0-88233-058-6 cloth
ISBN 0-88233-059-4 paper

Ardis Publishers
2901 Heatherway
Ann Arbor, Michigan 48104

Manufactured in the United States of America

for Marian, Yma and Yshélu

CONTENTS

Election

Exorcism

Viaticum

I

II

III

IV

highlife for caliban

election

Equilibrist

        (protocol for His Excellency)

an itch in the right
places, occasioning actual bodily
harm. a quarrel with people in
the right places

a dance of goose-stepping insanities to
shake shape out of our mouths
and a dream of carnage; now

that the wine fields grow softly
in the south of France; the tongue darts,
sips against the palate, rimming
the fluted edge of cups

and sweet white wines that wash
broken meat into our bones
in the right places.

A celebration in Istanbul

no man alive today can know which
side's dead men will win the war

I should have been here then.
south of Istanbul, I mean. squeezer of

concertinas to Cassandra the mad knowing
now in a book of numbers of other

men's dead men inside the belly of a
horse, waiting. to be alive and to

know the secret organ of pregnant wood hollow
with promise of precarious stones south

of Istanbul! to sit by the Dardanelles and
see which side's dead men push

stones away, raising the skull at the
sound of water in the Straits.

"Jericho is older than agriculture"

who indeed?
who, Rilke, if we screamed would hear
among the angelic orders?
silent as suspended flight Stalin sits,
cornerstoned, studies his latin grammar
who indeed in that immense victory of
latin grammar picks
the Ave from Gabriel's slow grammar

I know too a
Russian book that says
"you do not need to stand on chair
to look at floor"

I would advise then against the wagging of
elegant heads at singing tenors.
(against the grammar of castrati) some
say il signior Mussolini could sing
Ras Tafari Selassie upside
down and the high-pitched painter's moustache sniff
out hairs in the armpits of jews

Oh virginia, mater virgina,
in delusions of cowbells and roots
we chew off our legs to escape,

"Night in Casablanca"

(fantasy for men with power)

this much you did not promise:
the carving of well-
intentioned murders, the night turbulent with
sharp-nippled women soft-scripted
in Lisbon or, if you like,
Casablanca. it makes no difference which for
could you walk on water
you would —and so meet us there
Lisboa antigua or Casablanca

and men with precisely small moustaches
play in small or huge orchestras

there was rot at the center
but here one dances the feet to a last merengue
the short silk of night ladies cold
between the crotch

and a man with too much power, tip-toe with promise,
                                        prepares to
walk on water, as they say, unopposed.

His Excellency at Fort Thornton

(notes for an undelivered political speech)

if things could be that still-lifed.
hanging on walls
we would be stone-head companions
to Modigliani
or mannered
descend flowing staircases
with Picasso nude
in stiff-lined ecstasies.

stationed just so along woodwork and cornice.

a fortress of white stones on a small hill.

the Governor-General once lived here
an englishman, plumed.   in white flannels

who lived in large houses
needing more air.
the tropics being, as they are, the tropics.

at the top (they say)
a telescope swept the sky
for exploding stars
and their promise of cold gases

distilled in rain.

no goatherd of Genesis he;
he kept his counsel.
though some noticed Fort Thornton shaped

precariously like an ark.

but he kept his counsel and
neither in vegetable mineral or animal
did the ark take more than was decent.

some knew of an ark
but believed its boards rotten on another mountain
another sin. but believing in fire

we unthatched our houses
in time for rainstorms.

His Excellency: II

what does this man want?

that there are men with scottish blood
in Brazil
that is not so unthinkable

a broken fragment of portuguese makes hardwood lawful
and this, *madeira de lei,* is sayable
being thought

whatever we cannot say (having thought) shatters
                                    into loud image
sends the tongue probe probing the meat
of ikon. nails gleam into wood testing
the limit of wood. what
then to do with the cry that staggers at the root?

this man. *ecce homo.* for love
of whom some took kerosene lamps
to the water's edge. the dark edge of water.
and there learned

the sea teaches nothing but water.

so we picked burning kerosene, broke
skulls with one another,
vagrant calendars in which we saw marks,

and thought—
wished them diacritical.

the shapes of our skulls are now no different
than they were.   yesterday.   the day before yesterday?
did scattered bone plate
into image resisting image? but

now, this much is not so unthinkable

that here, *madeira de lei,* are incarnate
the limits of hard law and wood.

His Excellency: III

(in the first act)

a good man with a stick.

nothing here that teases Oedipus
out of a sphinx but,
plainly, a good man with a stick.

the dust rises and settles
into strange pregnancies in
these our violent hesitations

at crossroads.

our prayers invite flies. red
cloth at
crossroads falls into the
governance of a raging man, too

wise to go blind. though
stiff-faced they tap tap their
way—the blind grown wise—

tap
tapping their way. no man

chooses to live in hell.
therein lies the
fascination of hell in small places (a
narrow man gone to stick in
the first act.) the third

act waiting to forgive   .
rulers their odd invasions into the body
politic our mouths dance
in shreds in our faces.

the eye remains.

His Excellency: IV

pacem in terris

in Brazil the kreen-akrore rest in fear
of men with too much power.
and so they wait, these men,
in supplications of glass bead and axe.

the trees age. wet with rain that falls and falls.

what is it with us?

the night ordinary with visitors a
violin
leans far into the night in Bucharest

that Bucharest
should be capital to Rumania
what are these things to us here? (You
in your power and the rest)

that an italian man loving
latin
should write long and short words in latin

it is a coincidence of untidy passions in time
this:
that a dog wearing contact lenses be
killed by motor-car in Spain; where

Frederico Garcia-Lorca laid down before the Guardia
Civil and died.

and what is it to us?

we are not dogs, the
length of our teeth lost in foam though

we creep among mangrove shrouded creeks
a supplication of latin things about our necks.

His Excellency: V

(design for a house)

this picking away at the corner
of things!

I could make a very remarkable lunatic
for you. an especial dispensation
lacking exorcism.
                        design houses
for dandified dispositions swung
at the end of curved sticks. leather
crops even the seams of our blueprints.

a very remarkable lunatic and more
at fine coronations: lace-
bodiced ladies armed
with men in long-stemmed ambitions.
a summer, perhaps, in Prague
for compensation and

the ambitious burning of flesh in a public square.
and two gold pieces for justifications in
cyrillic script. coming, as they do,
cheap.

you understand, I am not now on the
verge of suicide. merely a
maker of conversations in certain keys;

an architect, like Arrabal, at odds
with strange emperors.

His Excellency: VI
(the reburial of Marshal Pétain)

they take them away at dawn
out of the broken earth the time
right to put them back in other holes in the earth.

No, these bodies will not tumble
out of strong coffins though
strawberries grow wild and tick and
grow to clock faces without hands.

we drag the eye to wooden windows
our biographies grown to rags
in the coffins of leaders going to

their reburials, having fallen;
and a temporary liberty lurks,
itself possessed of a terrible patience.

I speak now of death. not yours
—you in your numerous names
awaiting your going up—capable
as you are of resurrecting burials
along walls and quick cracking vaults.

devotions before Mass
yield us tentative loaves broken
in vichy water or water at Lourdes but

I speak now of death, ours,
stumbling as we do upon the white bone of power.

The alchemist & a most magical company

there will be the devil to pay,
we say; a most magical company
out of a ragged root.
                        below us a
man works at bellows and forge

but imagine now,
out of an inclination to
worry the wound, imagine a
most magical company of young men
with no addresses
                        and imagine too
that magic is a hard word
that explains nothing but magic

a man works hard at the navel of the earth
and all my friends go homeless.

Put your money

on zero
I would bow low, down
from the waist down
and so tranquilize the heart, ease
the warm desire
to eat human flesh
the corners of my lips raised
on zero

on perhaps this or that tedious day
inheritance is everything
bones a mere rattle

First Exorcism:
*This first time, he breathes gently on the
child's face three times, saying Latin
words that tell the unclean spirit to make way.*

Last Exorcism:
*The priest, before entering the baptistery,
for the last time exorcizes in Latin every evil spirit.*

The Missal

exorcism

Calypso for Caliban

this is the place
my inheritance
a chain of leached bones
my inheritance
mother
this
a chain of leached stones
airless quays
dust that rises
coasting on water

ah they walk on water
for you
they walk on water
papa prospero
papa legba
atibo legba
the whores
with water walk on water
papa prospero

jig me mama too
jig me mama
papa prospero jig
jig me mama
to born the beast

prospero
papa legba ah
him goin to make me

and thee
prosperous
to make the beast
white
him goin to kiss the whores
in she certain parts

ach Mother Mary
holy mama of God
pray for us
for us
for dem mamas with
derelict vaginas
defunct
not holy
to make the beast
with atibo prospero

keep the air
out of me mama's hole
let I choke
black
on air

ah! Virgin Mary
keep the carnival of Lent
the feast of ashes
in the dance
of the open thigh
the flexed knee while

black beasts
prowl
the pastures of my brain

atibo prospero ah!
papa prospero, sir,
dem whores put
black lips
on their private vaginas
sir

derelict
I prowl
these quays
dissatisfied with my face
prospero
against the face
prospero
of your daughter
prospero
prowling the fringes
of the tempest

Holy Mary
mother of God
Hail Mary
mother prey
the edges
of cane sugar
and cotton
pray here
at the beginning of
a new time:

I turn the corners of my eyes
to a vision of hulks
and black flesh
drugged in vomit and fart

the wind breaks
in derelict places
neither ariel
nor daughter
I grow dissatisfied
with this and that corner of my face.

Figures in wood

Captain want jig jig?
—**Heart of the Matter**

how indeed could we sink!
the gods stand up for bastards
(in their own odd dance)
falling out of the sky foreskins
peeled back

we could kneel on the sea
and not sink though the caked
hulls of ship, their ships,
departing, shake the wakes we intend
(or keep)

the earth too would refuse our weight
for we pass yellow water that digs holes
in the earth. we bear

responsibility even for thoughtless aims.
it makes no difference
that our piss is in a broken language:

small bottles and long-stockinged
scriptures litter the harbours. here

where cunt met dick
in simple enough english (though

not understanding the lingua franca
of those who trade, they called us
"simplified"). how indeed could we sink!

we bartered. unclear

[37]

what we won or lost. though

behind us we surely hear certain ladies,
lonely now on stone quays, eating
into their thighs (to the very bone) their
gaze seeking ship or chariot there.

Call us Ishmael (if you wish) or Barabbas
or Cain. we would barter too in coinage

and not sink.

the ports lie now in slack water
our fingers scrape the sides of empty bowls
and go back to our lips.

Highlife for traders

Under the spreading chestnut tree
I sold you and you sold me
                                    —Orwell

I

dem english take carvings
to Liverpool
germans take dem bombs
to Liverpool

bones in
a basket:
these
the faces
that peeked
and peered
slit out
of the meat
of wood

odudua he join them too
damballah he join them too
bones in a basket
when dem lie down
eshu
god of broken
penises he join
them too
ah what a carnival
them all dance!
took place
before them all
went
home again
home again
when shall I

see my native land
shall I never forget my home!

II

the thought
the thought
of getting up
then
entered sometimes
in our head
but it turned out
this way
easier
we joined wood
to wood built
comfortable
latrines
sat down our
mouths grown sour
sat down and
listened how,
far
down, our
colons
dropped
from us
turning into
tails
the heat
of maturing shit
hot
against the balls
cooked
them

[40]

dead

for lack
of proteins
it remained
for the feet
to cleave twice
into hooves

III

"ah,
much throatshaking!
this ere the
organs of increase
grow sour this
much I give:
item: spoons
of elephant teeth
item: 2 bags lead
balls
10 yards of
scarlet
scarlet
cloth
item: for a stout man
2 patna do two
bajudepants
two blue & one half cotton
item for a lean man
not sick
with pox
necanees two
two green ells two
lbs basons pewter

item: and yonder
wench
longbreasted
who coughed
my organ coasting
in oyle of palm
deep
yron works
of sundry sorts
manillios and bracelets
anklets of copper and
bracelets marked in portuguese
that much...

lord milord
much holding
of things done
in the heart's
core...
            besides,
the wench
milord is dead
is dead."

IV

not, we thought, the rooting
snouts
of hogs
the politics of the second coming.
thinking
it was chop—
ful
yellow in proteins
gold-plated

proteins
against starch:
garri and palm-
oil salt
and garri
garri and yam,
thinking
gold in protein
we laughed...
after all
"I chop
you chop
we all chop"
and oga
palaver finish
in the kingdom
we sought first

to-tee-o-to
water garri and salt

V

the present inhabitants
are a
black/
skinned
race of people
and dolichocephalic
prognathistic
and thick
with noses
and wooly hair
and lips and
thick with too much

lips/
skinned/
the present
my god!
the starched
khakies
of men
who groan
in latrines
who reach
rag in right hand
for the crust
of precise excrement
flaked dry
into dry gold.

A dance of pilgrims

my father, wheezing esthete,
before he died, giving
birth to me
and you, played
on pedal organs:
small-gaited pilgrimages,
peregrinations that
faded at odd crossroads
melodic lines moth soft
making broken winged flut-
ters
inside the crab
and the goat lines
that keep us here
at the equator

and so, my friend,
the baptism
and so, the sacrament
of penance playing
midwife to bad
consciences, aging
patterns
that make life here odd
the breadth of these harbors
with their names: free-
town, gold/coast/and ghana
ivory/bight of benin/coast
once cool estuaries
chuffing with image:

II

St. Francis of Assisi
spoke
to small birds
who small-stepped it to
his austere
rock, falling
out of the sky, sky-
flesh stretched in
eager anticipation of stone

there was a time
a year ago or
was it ten
(already?) the architects
thinking of herons
being bigger birds, the
architects
stood on one foot
in deep waters believing
the other foot safe.

having believed.

III

it is never autumn
or winter spring or
summer here
the two-toned dry
visitation or wet
of nature is our inheritance,
lumbering
pas de deux visits that
mirror

our tight wisdoms:
the heat
driving us indoors
the rains
driving us indoors where
our voices
angled against the equator
we think Kew gardens and
Browning, the eve bitter cold
against St. Agnes

the seasons right we go
(one foot quiet against
our navels)
on pilgrimages.

for having believed then
men love to go on pilgrimages.

Prodigal's canticle

caduceus

from beyond
the edge
I recall these things
craters

dutch castles
and
stones
marked in portuguese

three stones
in
wet ashes
gray
stones iron
stones
in gray ashes

the fires
dead
dead
meat of
fowls
in pots iron
pots

standing
on
three legs
on

three stones
dead.

ku omo jade
but now
at the cratered
center blue-
clotted the
meat of cow
neither fat
nor fatted

(the narrow
tongues of
serpents flick/
erring
back into
crooked stick in
my travelling hands)

II

oh for stately ships
winged
galleons gliding
to lie
with water in
clean
harbors the
waters lap
lapping
in blue
coves the
coves wet
with water the

ships riding
blue in
sky-water

travelling

III

avatar

it is not
out of the question
for fires to
lie
dulcent among
the plains out-
cropping rocks snap-
ping against
the sun

avatar of
light-headed malignancies
bruised
into the heads
of charlatan lions

bloated into
the smell of
dogs

the roads rocky.
steep.
dog teeth
in the stick of
those who
return
travelling

[50]

IV

awoojoh

"*ku omo jade*
bring him out
we did not come
merely to set
teeth
against the
hard edge of iron

ku omo jade
the smell of
saliva lingers
still on our
fingers ashes
in the far corners
of our
mouth.

there are words
to be
pitted in the ears
of the
rock-bound: you,

the son, who
see
have seen, stick
in hand, tell

about

the succulent
passages of fine
women leaning into the

riot of living flesh

of those who set
the teeth
at the root of tree
mountain fire
water air
and earth con-
tending: the

rage and
riot of substance."

V

and I come to
myself
drumming
a canticle of dry
sticks

travelling.

Vèvè

vèvè
ouvre
vèvè
ouvre le bayé
you got
to lift the gate

eh hen
madioment en hen

the sun
falls
like
the moon
falls
on the man
and his rock

at the top
at the bottom
eye-
ball with
blood
eh hen
madioment en hen

faut imaginer
eh hen
blood wash-
ing
the living

[53]

bone
eh hen
faut imaginer
cet homme
madioment
Sisyphe est
heureux at

the bottom

a wheeling
stranger
a stranger
of everywhere
and
here

and *eh*
hen
extravagant
at
the top the
eye-
ball filled
with blood
eh hen

Covenant

I would descend quickly to bone
though
the lower world's shudder bruise
my picked shanks

Baron Samedi
keeper of bones
bone setter: I would descend
smartly acolyte
of bone. setting this bone
in dance against that. this pelvis
of gaping bone
bone-dry
against the shudder
of the world's epicenter

pick
my skull
clean
of meat; pick
the bones
of the uterus
clean
of meat against
the grace
of breaking waters

I would descend quickly

pick

clear
geometries of repose
opalescent hieroglyphs
of bones
against the quivering
hunger of
earth-eating rodents

neophyte of bone
I descend

Witchdoctors

disbelieving in the accidental
we came warily enough.
with raffia brooms
this other one
with bamboo whistles, power
against witchcraft; for
ease of strange sicknesses
goatskin pouches. so
we came to walls that leaned in
frantic eagerness
toward the atlantic

you remember now there
was a man, who clung to the
sides of mountains,
gray as granite
a lover of laterites
a believer in stones, he
tottered among stones smashing
at our passage
the sides of mountains
into gray hair

you remember now an ivory man
whose hammer marked the terms
at michaelmas
at trinity
at epiphany but he too believed

in stones an
ivory man of gray ashes

he fought his way into mountains.
a lover of stone tablets he
talked of wooden dogs
with nails, protection
against water.

you remember we grew older,
our skulls distended. and you remember
we came down
to meet our fates, playing
fauns in passage through mountains.

the bows are bent back.
the arrows sing flute-swift.

we grew to be older;
the arrows singing their way.

a vague man leaps among our mountains
maddened with granite.

Juju

do you remember? the words
in their especial candor.
madame northway laid hands on beggars
de-veined us; madame northway, conjugating
love of St. Augustine out of the iron
heat of the equator over our heads,
non amabat, did not love; but then
loving to love, sed amans amare, seeking
querens amare to love beyond our windows and
the smell of black buttocks rubbing raw
faeces on the barks of trees. seeing that
paper was scarce among us. and rags were
needed to keep inquisitions of a too
curious nature from our bones
blackened with lust of St. Augustine
and Carthage burning.

and the marvel of that little white
english woman. the delicate white
hairs of feminine moustache, filming
face into mouth-covering dendrites:
a hollow-tubed anemone opening—

against the reign of the beast
rising out of our empty harbors—
her teeth small-white

so she flicked out conjugations of love
and drove us mad.

our buttocks grow raw on the barks of trees.

the trees themselves are black smooth, with
faeces cracking inward to join the flow of sap.

but papers; ah! the alphabets of empires met
outside. in the dry seasons of our windows:
the tambourines of Byzantium
moist skulls under stone in Rome
do you remember? Cartago delenda est?
the bone dust of sicilian mountains
growing green with bees and honey and vergil

how then could we use paper? papers
round as rosetta stones. and heavier.
between our windows and ourselves.

how then could we squat anywhere else
but under our own trees
and leak things into the sap of our trunks.

Exorcism

(for Miss Elizabeth Hirst)

I

narrow
as a calvinist's ark
this too
is the place
built for us
by strangers

my ears hinged
back
against my head
I listen
for there has been
a death

why else
would old photographs
turn yellow
against the walls

why else
would glass
refuse
our reflection
turning
to the wall

II

the split
meat
of sunflower
seeds satisfies

but only hunger
of a certain age

the sun
under my tongue
blue
as a goat's
I shall be gallant
to titian-
eyed ladies
besotted
with madrigals;
lean
against the
far corners
of all Gaul
divided
drawing lines
under words
videre licet
it is permitted to see

brother
when that april
with his showers sweet
the drought of March
pierces

III

a stake
in the center
of my head
let me grind
even in

sleep, when it comes,
bone
against bone
the prayer
and the curse
tight
behind my teeth
believing
nothing but
the black
water (once my
eye)
seeking passage
to my throat

I grope
in my narrow
cave for
things
in the underbellies
of sheep

flies eat
at the broken
edges
of the sun's eclipse

the sound of
paddles
beating against
sea water
for ten years
penelope
waiting

but they go
the sun
visible
and
Penelope waiting

the ships
too far
the rocks
too heavy

IV

chaste
as rock
against spume
let me bleed
creeping
my knees raw
up
Mount Athos
sard and
chrysoprase
in spume
KHALKIDIKI
KHALKIDIKI
O my friends
I have such longings
creeping
up
Mount
Athos
I would mouth
such fat phrases
as would

tickle
the ear of Lazarus
dulcis
dulcis
in hora mortis
while black goats
crop
the brown earth

O my friends
I would dance
ecstatic
in my narrow cell
but at Mount Athos
the world fallen
down
the rotten sides
of
steep stone

et quondam paupere
cum Lazaro
quondam paupere
aeternam habeo requiem
quondam paupere

set upon
by wishes
not my own.

V

set upon
I grope,
plough teeth

back into roots

cum Lazaro

adsum!
set upon
the voice
that cleaves
the maggot marrow
of the brain

let his head
be
beaten
upon grinding
stones

to sift
blood
from the black earth

let his head
be
beaten
upon grinding
stones

to gather
small bones
together

adsum
against
the din

to gather
small stones
polished
white
cushioned in rot
my eyes
gone

I come
dulcis.

set.
the moon
sucked.
my eyes
bone-white.

dulcis
dulcis

Shylock, after

"condamnamus te
ad vitam
diaboli
vitae"

my cap
on my skull
they
have condemned
me

my cap
against
my skull
the shakers
of clever jaw-
bones
immaculate
against the night.

on such a night
"what is different
about this night."

condamno te
condamnamus te
in nomine
by name you the jew
I the jew
my gabardine the jew
condamno

[68]

ad diaboli

jessica
jessica keep
the windows
that the pipes
and the recorder
and the flute
whistle only
against the seamed
edges of my skull
cap

jessica
in gehenna
"as of the fool
there is no remembrance
forever" as of the wise

I am cramped
against the night
condamnatus
sum by
farters in silk
silk...
"baptized though
there will ever
be larceny
in your heart

the blast
of furnaces
the furnaces
of alchemists in

your nose
long in yellow
usury
your jewish gabardine
yellow
the dry joints
of your touched
hips touched
like the thief's
at beth-el
clinks yellow
the eyes of the "jewish dog"
are yellow
gold that
trap the light
in this
the city of God
in usury
and yellow
lust, burning

ergo
condamnamus
condamnamus
te
te
baptizo
ergo
in nomine
by name the jew
sed semper
the jew
golem in yellow
gold pax
tecum."

and the earth is not flat
and the earth has no steep sides
        against this
the dropping of things
gathered together
in the obscure heart of the world
golem in gold
golem in
the city of God
golem golem
I hold a blazing
faggot
against the shakers
of jawbones
with yellow teeth

jessica
jessica in
gehenna
for a wilderness of
monkeys in
gehenna

my feet are sandalled
against this
the penultimate
open razor
of history

"what is different
about this night?"

against
the beginning

of peace
I hold a blazing faggot
against
the ovens of gehenna.

In Ashanti, God left man, they say, because an old woman repeatedly jolted him with her pounding stick. Then one day God said, "Because of what you are doing to me I am taking myself far up into the sky."

viaticum

Viaticum

(for Eliseo do Bomfin)

scented daphnes and dust will have their day

behind us
are those with whom we read *o estado do sao paulo*
our teeth chilled to crystal
cups in that living room in manhattan

and eliseo plays, favelado,
with a minimum of nail in the right-
hand fingers
                        Yemanja, ialorixa
                        deixa di tristeza
                        ten pena da mi

and in the corners dr haddim tadashi
whose shaved head talked into the night
about amnesty for jews in soviet prisons

here, in the center, the acid
perfumes of badly douched women who
sit cross-legged at cocktails

eliseo plays with a minimum
of nail in the sky on sixty-sixth
street & amsterdam eating at condominiums

smooth as white jade.

these things leave a bruise in the heart.
outside the cold cracks like a whip

wild geese feint paths over the edge of the sky
and fly south

when the wind dies down we leave for home.
below us
the continent surprises: brown earth
edging the white smooth tips of the southern atlantic.

San Rafael

at aix
we tucked napkins under our chins
sitting at side-walk cafes, read Eliot
and called them "estaminets" a fresh elitism
between our teeth

madame, at roc *fleuri,*
likes the japanese, we sit raw-boned,
rice paper walls between us

art teachers tell us of
chromatic anxieties: sunbursts
and etched crows in the ears
of dutch painters

the expectations of soviet jews
such as we read them, are different:
"they said you didn't buy eggs in Isra-el
they said they simply lay about in the street"

to the south
lies san rafael
in reefs of white water;
we slake our thirst on fine-grained sand
farther out, the sea is an alarming blue.

provence is (after all) not recklessly beautiful
we return
the doors to our rooms austerely closed.

Pan at Christmas

a syntax of yellow barricades
hangs between your speech and mine
but ah! keep them away, the tits
of your short or long limbed women.
keep them from open spaces when
hoofs strike and
the seamless phrases of the flute
strike through the stones
of this or that town

my dreams are corniculate, and
tit for tit
would set you again to bethlehem
for no real purpose.

Coronation

Oh, how willingly I would give up
all the women of the world to
possess the mummy of Cleopatra
—*Flaubert*

metaphors stammer around them
these girls
laméd into white leather and
gold skins

what are they to me who
would wish on them
whatever dances in my head?

they sit
no matter the time of the month
they sit straddling

the necks of long-trousered men.
what are they to me?
in their season

no matter the angle of sun or moon
they will descend again,
straddling thighs yoked to carriers.

though I skirt them
they resist translation keeping
to themselves the secret mechanisms

of Midas' gold-soft passage.

and the burnished throne empty.

Ophelia at Elsinore

a cylinder of mud rots
in the space between ophelia's thighs
and rotten rots
the place where the prince of denmark
thought to lay his head

the sea is not given to
excitements such
as vex the bones of mammals

and ophelia rots in a hole
as though she were hardened
against her young ones, as though
they were not hers, which
in fact they are not, being
in fact denied her, being
in fact denied the passion of old men
rat-skewered behind stained sheets
being denied
the rapier-sheathed thrusts of
princes who dig
worms into the cold ecstasy of old
men who,
worms between their tired shanks
peep and
clutch at forbidden points

because God deprived her of wisdom
because God walked on water not

wearing the petticoats of crazy spinsters;
and ophelia
lightly lightly walking
on water
in petticoats
in the year of the Lord
turned her face from the sun to
gather the stuff of seaweeds
and mud
in the holes between her eyes
and nose
in the holes between her teeth
and lap
deadening the holes under hairs
into which
a voice, politely impolitely, once said:
"lady, shall I lie in your lap."

Fragments

stabat mater
judica me mater
though I would have you know
I seek no permanent residence
in these matters

though I skirt the stone paths
of gardens
avoid the sound of footsteps
on gravel-
rocks that trap the moon
in pieces of silver
reflected off the sounds of footsteps
running
against
white
stones

stabat.

the time ripe
you gave birth with ease
the days noisy with the palm and the ass
to the fabulous
junk
that gleams
disincarnate
in the cellars
of our minds

woman, I would not

beat
my head
upon stones
till I die
like a dog
till dogs
eat of the flesh
thereof.

between
the kissers
between the bather
of the feet of lepers
and one
named
Iscariot
man of Kerioth
was a game
played
to the bone

woman, I would have
you
know I
would not now
strike
the skull
(played out
to the bone)
against
the sifting
of things
in stone-
graves already empty

a waste of breath
against
teeth
locked
in the
passing kiss
of one man
to another

a waste of breath
to cough
out the lungs
against
the crowing
of cocks
who crow
the morning
and the evening
of the third
day (and other days)
seeing
that it is good...

stabat
mater.
judica
virgina
et discerne

though
woman,
I would have you
know...

The devil at Wantagh

(for Ruth)

> The night my father got me
> his mind was not on me.
> —*Housman*

I have come through concentric circles
to this,
the place

no white-bone antlers sprout
in my hair
though at my passage cows lick out
deformed calves in afterbirths

though your father, coins in his eyes,
paces over head on wooden beams
(and the waters are warm
between the corners of your blue-white legs)

there are bones in my private parts
you will not be big with child;
though this is not a promise.

State of grace

           (Notre Dame de Paris)

a slight change of plans

and Lucifer is past titillating.
his tongue, by force of stone
merely, hangs erect at Notre Dame.

but you.

you wish,
mon ami, to zou zou
avec our ladies of Paris

and you set then a not
too difficult proposition.
though in a company of acrobats,
playful,
gargoyles have crept up
our stones, their tongues dry. here,
over this city,

a sad singing of hymns.
Our Lady washes her stones
in a black river.

water flows into clean basins at
Monmartre. the girls wash
their quick thighs. once more.
and descend the stairs again to
where you wait with tourists

always with tourists (ces gens

[86]

du nord!) but you wait and

the water laps
cleanly in clean basins.

Venice

it's this I remember the most

the train clattered out of Milan
the men inside our compartment scratch their groins

on the vaporetto i signiori veneziani erect
forefingers in palms wondering how
well you (blonde of hair) and I did it.

there are fishbones in Venice
and the screams of urgent cats

small streets lead us to gondoliers called Pavarotti
water sucks at the rotting stones of hotels

we do not give birth with ease:
I am not tempted to death by water
and you, sedate, keep your thighs.

Galapagos Island

turtles in heat snap-
ping
at other turtles
in heat

ill-grace at Galapagos
dragging pain and
ecstasy into warm water

eggs breaching sand.

white-spanned
the gulls swoop, elated
stylists of air

between hard shells
and air, mining liquid
gold out of sand

though turtles live longer.

the gulls need the gold of eggs
to spin dizzy parabolas
swift-sided

and to tilt sideways
in death, the turtles
dragging out the tired cunt
of females against the years.

Senghor at Christmas

> I'm putting a curse on you...may your
> children lick the ass of your gods' enemy."
> —Junkwoman *(Ain't Supposed
> to Die a Natural Death)*

things have come to this
once out of axis
it's difficult to lick one's own elbows
merely to prove a point

this morning (being Christmas)
my daughter met
Jesus
at St. Andrews stone church
(it being Christmas at St. Andrews, also)
Mary's son (yellow of hair)
defying carnality
my daughter
being four
and no Santa Teresa

II

I remember
seven years ago (at Christmas)
a bolivian indian, exiled,
and I
pursued Verdi across the susurrating squeals
of goodyear tires—
because her name was Aida—

it seemed a good enough reason.

I remember she had a sister
named
Maria Choquetaxi —broad of cream-gray

teeth, in her eyes and beyond,
the multifoliate wisdoms of
visiting
        arche/anthro/pologies—

it seemed a good enough reason
(at the time)

to compare
lean
Verdi
antiphons
in dirty rooms

and she,
rounding the corners of her menopause.

III

now, at Christmas,
at thirty-one and a little,
never having built
snowmen from white crystals,
my daughter and I rush out,
thinking it easy.

Attention please

          (canticle for Emily Dickinson)

I carry my soul quietly
a little to the left under
my left ear sometimes
when the wind cracks across leaves

the forefinger and thumb
of my left hand can reach at a whip
a soul that hangs like a kernel
of dry meat there, at the end of picked scabs

I have taken to sleeping
on my left side, reaching
between hard gum and probing tongue
for dry kernels such as end
even the succulent breasts of the blessed.

Letter to my tailor

(London)

the human mind, it's true, survives
all but its own hanging.
lately I have taken to walking
with my elbows close to my body

if you like, you may say
I do not like the climate or again
you may say, if your like, you may say
"he has taken twelve stitches inside
the corners of his mouth, his
elbows keep the rebellion of brittle
bones polite"

here in their season
I have nothing against the jaws
of steam shovels eating into the corners
of henrietta street

               no.
I have recently taken to french trousers
with buttons on a long fly; being,
lately, in no hurry to ease myself.

Horus to Joseph

tell me in what part of the woods flowering
in agapanthus and wild watsonias
you would dally with me. my
firstborn dead. the
waters are blood
a hail of frogs eats
away the corners of lily pads and Thebes

it's a long time since these things
calyx krater and smooth marbled
satyr keep company with alarms in museums

the bands grow brown in Ramses' face
his face, and yours, stiffen into surprised bone
and cave

it's a long time since the stream-fed
son of Ramses' daughter pulled back the wand—
and chariots and others under the sea to the east—

those who came back then
came back

I stiffen my neck beyond the gaze of visitants
in the bottom floors of museums.
I am content to be nothing but
stone-smooth stone figure calm
with the head of a bird.

Timeo danae

I fear
for the greeks

the greeks ask for Byron's body and
for their asking get his lungs
heavy with sea water

et
dona ferentes:
the etiquette
of things
that ride
lightly on surf and spume
indifferent in gift.

Armistice

The train whistles past lizards on the plateau at Jos
we cross the bridge near Kafanchan

below, on the Mojhoya-Dji, the paddles of wooden steamers
break up bamboo lotuses on magic water
bright water drips from the loin cloths of crab fishermen

at Kaduna indigo tunics have left dyes on naked long-nippled women
they wave; the train speeds

wheels shatter hard coals about our eyes
the smell of iron and rough ashes breaks in our nostrils

the train speeds; we have put cut sandalwood
on the coffins we carry north.

The king of a distant country (1940-44)

a memory at 78 rpm

those who came back talked.

of bone-cracking ecstasies
on flat breasted women in wooden shoes.
of small muscled people with too much fat
under the eyelids but who, they saw,
saw clearly enough;

others
for the ragged enthusiasms of flesh
ate sand in boneyards.
quietly

they took ships for Burma.
liking the british.

and they took ships for Burma
liking the clack of mahjong tiles
rapid calligraphies
in trenches

and the king in a distant land
they took to ships;
liking too the reckless moustaches of
strangers in starched khakies.

it will come, you say,
and this much I say, the adjourned

promise in baroque radios

[97]

we did not invent will come
Marlene Dietrich's black knickers
the drone of jew's harps
in the delicate mouths of beggars, the
cliffs white over Dover, the
king in a distant country

and you in stiff attentions, the
fields ripe in poppy days,
Dietrich in song and me saying now

my father's latest radio (surely)
was a voice kissed by God.

The brigadier-general's dance

(for Kwame Nkrumah)

> The coup ended with the hangings at 3,4,5, and 6 a.m.
> of four men. Going first was the brigadier-general who
> spoke impeccably but gave much trouble.
>
> Sierra Leone, 1971

at Rokupr
the dry
season's dry-red soil
our witness

we buried his useless testicles,
tight in retreat
from his broken neck

the idea, though,
at Rokupr
was to "interrupt"
in measured drop
the western extension
of the brigadier-general's neck

that we did too—
at three a.m.—
the insolence of imagistic rains
our witness.

laterite millstones
under Rokupr
preserve the ochre-
caked
scrotum
of the brigadier-general

II

perched,
toe-tipped,
in Toronto
Nureyev, corsetted,
insists:
close-up lenses
capture sweat
(perhaps sweatsmells too)
not Tschaikowsky
over trapdoors

> "I would much prefer
> the circumstances these
> you do not come close"   and

long shots
full-bodied
in Toronto watch
lean meat under
tutus
of clitoridectomied ballerinas
retreat
allegretto (ma non troppo) from
the
corsetted center of
the
brigadier-general's thigh tremors

III

the eyes of trapdoors,
wise Nureyev,
are caveats anent
the exits of dons Juan
and Nijinsky

we,

for our part,
are uncertain if
the brigadier-general saw
his legs, skin-tight,
                    leap
to
 Gounod;
Tschaikowsky being too long a name
for the swift
crack of neck
bones; the
pointless
diastolic
andantinos of
heart muscles
                —after the fact.

Robben Island

(after Sheik Amidou Kane)

civilization is after all merely
the architecture of our response to history:

before the earth understood
what Copernicus knew it stood
still while, for instance,
men at Sodom or Gomorrah
put delicate mouths to each other
and licked off fires

while, for instance,
somebody's wife cracked into salt
and the seventh frequencies of horns
cracked the walls of this or that city

for those of us
fashioned,
to live on the backs of others
the exaltation of ram
horns holds few testaments

On Robben Island, for instance,
shy wardens have been known
to look away
while urinating into the mouth
and scattered teeth of prisoners.

[102]

Economy of cloth

One must not underestimate the advantage
for a writer of having a mad wife at home.
—*Signior Barzini*

it was not art. nor
indeed considerations of art that
kept the tails of our shirts flying
to flap back
against our naked buttocks

our crotches dry

nor was it a suggestion of art
the things that left us untrousered;

untrousered, less weighty our
private parts like black bells
beating the head of meat
against the meat of the thigh

the end was neither music nor flight
our crotches dry.

grown wiser we take interest
in cloth. grown wiser, three-
quarters of all hats are made in Mexico, a
book teases, wrong-headed; Xochicalco under
foot the pyramids dry under foot

the earth holding a
tilt in patience.

headkerchiefs of women, the time
right, do service

[103]

between their thighs and washed
return to the head
close to bone

and grown close to bone small
men grow short in china a
promise of rice field and small
book shaped into impatient pyjamas.

here, this one
walking
built sandals out of tyres.

here, to this other a god gives
confusedly
what was asked in fine clarity

the lips between her thighs pendulously tired
balaram pandurang wadkar's wife gives birth.
to one more child from a rope bed and
the sun continues, patiently, to burn the earth
our crotches hang tidy,
fringes of our landscapes

and this other one, dressed in old iron,
saw windmills
and wanted to fight them, seeing,
for love of self, he
was dressed in old iron against a too
economical dispensation of grace
neither wifed nor wifing.

A. T. & P. (Ltd.)

it's difficult these days
to recall what dreams we had.

the Africa Timber and Plywood Company
built us backless benches

the planed edges of which we sat
on making faces with Tarzan at negroes

sans-culottes
penis-sheathers

who, hungry,
probe for the colons of starving hyenas
who, sated,
belched between their thighs
who, it being time,
took Tarzan's spear deep in the throat
who, it being time,
turned their eyes to Jane
who, arms-akimbo,
walked open-legged over their eyes
who died
the wet juice of Jane's pubic hairs
edging paradise

and we,
we filed our teeth
sat back on our benches to wait

when, for our hospitality,
he gave us a negress
we killed and ate her.

Bamboo-ribbed sails

we wait, long lipped
under delicate antimacassars

were there not rice shoots and stone paths here
we'd sip green teas
eat the meat of force-fed fowls

al-Mukhlit

there are those of us who,
having shaved the insides of
our nostrils and ears,sit down
to food   for which
there exists no known botanical names

for a mithkal
we pushed rotten logs
where the river
coughed in a dry season

the upper reaches
of the river curve away
from long-jointed minarets
the scales of fresh-water fish are in our clean nostrils

here, Djenne smells like a drowned lake
there are dead fishes among the roots of bamboo trees
the red eyes of hungry lepers search among broken pots
for the cooked necks of partridges.

there are no deltas in the plains
but leeches reach the head waters:
ochre-colored lithams dry out the heads of the mixers
the muezzin leans over the dead stones of the river

in december the harmattan blows cold sand
our grey fingers keep warm inside the grey bellies of fish
there are small scales floating to the deltas
on the thin red entrails of the dead.

Split fences

masalik al-Jinan:
god has his saints, it is true.

men have (they tell us) lit fires on the moon
there are ashes on the roofs of our houses

here, the earth turns the wrong way
rivers wash the veins out of dry mountains

our temptations lie in grass blades
we have been known to forget the smells of water

here, the earth turns the wrong way
and leaves us the smells of women in winding sheets

our expectations are modest:
we search the verses of the dead son of Abdullah
                                    bin Abdul-Muttalib

we pick at sores, they heal.
there is silence between our teeth.

or

we talk about things we already know
our tongues are tufts of carded wool.

Immigrants

I

my head is bothered by passing footsteps under
                                        tangerine trees
I wheel hoops of discarded british bicycles

the spokes trap grains of sand; they sweep dry whispers
inside the circles of my flight:

there are growths between my thighs.
the cup of my left hand keeps them from my path.

I keep my face, an intermediate nuisance
in a bone-bright season.

II

here, the earth does not get fat.
that much we learn from the camels' cough.
it has not rained
few of us remember when it last rained.

it's flies that mate on the dried spit
we cannot swallow at ramadan.

few of us die.
we rub curds from the Fulbe on corpses
the smell of burning flesh breaks from half-finished
                                        faces.

we ululate and keep dogs away from those we burn.
there is no wind.

the wind blows but we carry inside our shaved heads
the explosions of flesh and wood.
here, when it rains it will shatter our houses.

Ablution

I will tether the canoe to a river willow
the river is full
crested cranes fly banking against the moon
shadows remain on the paddles of washerwomen

here is silent water
in the broken sides of conch, pink-white.

Visas

the americans are mad, of course; exist
among other things to wreck the delicate
phrases of our british tutelage

history hangs loose here for
ten american cents she winks
behind slotted cages

>   "the real Jeremiah Johnson killed two
>   hundred & forty seven Crow
>   Indians & ate their livers"

from beyond morningside heights those
of my colour come in
narrow lapels and narrow brimmed hats
slanted
dangling in dance like empty clothes
on meat hooks

for twenty-five american dollars
the warwicke hotel gives angular visions
of those
inside whose heads eggs
are laid and broken

down in the hotel's toilet
my children and I urinate with ease
for ten cents against white porcelains

we get enough paper
to keep piss drops from the flaps of our trousers
from my daughter's knickers

though my wife's breasts are small and untaxed
though my color falls apart in my hands
and the soles of my feet are blond
I keep to myself
avoid the beer-flavored orgasms of men
in ironed trousers
in tight hats here
in new york city I
await flight patterns hanging
in new york city by
fingertips to my skin.

Shopping list

(for my children who believe they are black
because they/we are used, not new, people)

the notice
having come in by mail (also)
I shall buy hair from
parucca di roma   new hair
that is   smooth-slick   gold
like fish streaking for deep waters
at the edge of the mediterranean

things would be easier.

matthew   it seems is
the boy down the street who
wants to play with my children

matthew knocks against the glass
panels
keeping the wind out of my house

his yellow hair catches the sun
sends
it
bouncing
across the refracted prisms of my house
springs back
against the artifacts that give shape
to the walls

I keep the panels of glass
between matthew   who wants
it seems

to play with my children
and myself

though he eyes the cracked nails
of my naked feet
the glass   being between us   he
cannot hear what I hear from the inside
that his hair is
the wrong color   that
his sire's hair
is the wrong color   that
the color is the wrong
type. he sees either the patterned
cracks on my toes or
a man with different hair
speaking in tongues
across panels that keep the winds
at the edge of the morning sky.

Feb. 14 & the bed of the king of france
(or the future is in potatoes)*

I

(code of conduct)

this scene adds nothing to the plot
this scene adds nothing to an understanding
of the character of the king of france

the shards of broken heads
tonight are jazzily   easily
cacophonous tonight   three
black men/
         under stress/
             have
been shot, in proportion, by
three policemen
        under stress   some
in yarmoulkas some & others
in pork pie hats
others in soft hats
others constructing
hats under stress: stereophonic
shooters of double-barrelled
speech
and explanations   attached to
a left ear &
to a right ear

---

*(all blacks agreeing to re-incarnation as potatoes)

this is not   repeat is not   the song of perforated livers
and impolite bullets under stress
in the ears of undertakers

when naked girls   leaking with too much seed
leave the bed of the king of france
this scene adds little to an understanding
of the character of the king of france

II

on february fourteenth a jenny-
ass gorilla humped in nebraska by a jack-
assed gorilla give birth in denver
to baby valentino   at the zoo   who
was born was dead was buried unrinsed
who dropped dead with too much water
in the nose
who dead saw his private parts turn to
skin-wrinkled potatoes under stress
of earth   such as delight the heart
in idaho
who dead   was diced   was sliced in boiling oil
and rose again to become french
to be eaten in bedrooms and in the rooms
of the living with breaded fish or
deep sliced livers leaking oil   keeping the
probe of probing fingers wet with thick juices
sucked at the mouth
in the bed of the king of france.

Children's choice

(in memoriam: T. I.)

I grant you this. once
there was a way to get back home.
but now there is deep love
of dead men to be loved safely:

breakfast and the sun rising early
on the tired cries of frog and cricket

my father first died
quietly enough and I
shall love dead men in retrospect

the egg, hardboiled,
slick-white
in the froth of your spit; as
your brain caved in on itself.

may white termites keep far from
the idle mockery of your coffin

may your white gloved hands crossed just so
hold down the passion of chest bones

may you keep to yourself
even the delicate cartilage of your nose
against the work of maggots
and the weight of stones

and should you lose
may your face when found
be buried in the earth again.

Protocol for a death at age forty-five

I do not now pace backyard fences
bone-prefixed
to chicken tract grafitti about
this or that loss

old women limp beyond me
coughing up their livers in small pieces
on frozen plains

the deranged underwears of changing
old men   change   merely to plug
the leakages of private griefs

let them.

I would die removed
from even the long-wristed tremors
of players on stradivariuses
who keep their lives tidy
with taut strings

I piss a strong colour   yellow
as an angry moon   a cup
of turtle blood hardens
whatever stains the cold front of my trousers

let   at this pacted age when
flesh begins to weary of being packed
thick to crisp cartileges
and uncracked bones that leak nothing

let   whatever tumors come
develop in my left armpit
and in my right armpit

I am not now
nor ever was   one
to kick the heels   clap
the palm smartly   over
the head   a flamenco dancer
with public armpits

I die keeping the cancers away
from the rattling of my voice

I do not empty my voice
in phlegm clot and bedpan

I ride vector and virus
to a standstill
stiffen against my wife's empty womb
my children asleep in the next room.

Quasimodo's bolero

a drum coughs inside the hollow
spaces of my back   whose
circumference of concave bones
hangs deaf

the bells ring bronze and iron
it is the fat of metal
that shivers in shocks of ecstasy
through the open spaces
of my rags
                    I
am companion to bells and gargoyles
whose rough sinews I pull into the cupped
orifice of my hands

I gag   convulsive swinger
on the erect clappers
of iron bells bronze bells

my back swells in the company of
bells & gargoyles   I pull on
rough ropes and iron tongues
copper tongues

my sometime six-inch penis leaks
stale water below me   my legs
and the bottoms of my feet fly
over flagstones   there are black fields
below   black with faeces   with

the stale faeces of the fertile
I receive into the flying orifice of my naked
buttocks the wind that is broken in
the corners of sacred places   and
my back swells with the noise of breaking wind
and the urgency of bronze and iron
copper and iron   giving birth
to a dance of concave bones.

NOTES

16 - Istanbul. The ruins of rebuilt Troy lie south of Istanbul

19 - Fort Thornton. Pre- and post-Independence State House in Freetown, Sierra Leone.

21 - *Madeira de lei.* Literally, "wood of law"; hardwood (Portuguese).

23 - Red cloth. Acts of propitiation frequently involve the wrapping of food etc. in red cloth *(sahrah);* this is then left at a crossroad.

25 - Kreen-Akrore. An Indian tribe still in hiding (at this writing) in the rain forests of Brazil.

33 - Atibo Prospero.
Papa legba.   "Atibo" as in "atibo legba" in voodoo; and "eshu elegba" in Yoruba mythology, where he is a god of mischief and malice: "We are singing for the sake of Eshu/ he used his penis to build a bridge/ the penis broke in two/ the travellers fell into the river."

37 - Figures in wood. Graham Greene's *Heart of the Matter* is set in Freetown, where it was also partly written. Greene was there during the war years. West African harbors were much used during World War II.

39 - Odudua. Damballah. Yoruba god of creation; supreme serpent god of Dahomey.

39 - *Home again.* The West African soldier's equivalent of "When Johnny comes marching home"/ "White cliffs of Dover."

41 - Scarlet cloth. "It was the scarlet which did for the Africans ... the Negro has always liked scarlet. It was the fault of this color that they put them in chains and sent them to Cuba." —Esteban Montejo, *Autobiography of a Runaway Slave.*

43 - Kingdom. "Seek ye first the political kingdom." —Kwame Nkrumah. In 1958 there was much promise.

43 - Garri. A basic West African food: flour made from the dried root of the cassava plant. West African food is for the most part heavily carbohydrate.

43 - "I chop." Chinua Achebe thus conjugates massive corruption in *A Man of the People.* Pidgin English - "chop": food, to eat.

43 - *To-tee-o-to.* Fragment of a children's song about recklessness.

48 - Prodigal's canticle. Rituals, e.g., the ceremonial feast at the first public presentation of a child, form the basis of the poem. *Ku omo jade* - bring the child out.
Awoojoh - ritual feast and food.

48 - Dutch castles....portuguese. The coast of West Africa is dotted with such memorabilia of the slave trade. The Portuguese named Sierra Leone—land of the lion mountains. The hills encircling the harbor seeming, to them, like two lions facing each other.

53 - *Vève.* The complex ritual marks made on the floors of voodoo temples at the start of worship.

54 - Sisyphe. "Il faut imaginer que Sisyphe est heureux"—one must believe that Sisyphus is happy. —Camus, *The Myth of Sisyphus.*

56 - Baron Samedi. In voodoo, Petro cult, Lord of the Cemetery, Maker of Zombies.

59 - Juju. In West Africa, magical power; sometimes in the form of amulets, charms, etc. This power may be harnessed for good or evil.

61 - Exorcism. When there is a death in the house, all pictures and mirrors are turned to face the wall. The spirit of the deceased is thus protected from seeing himself and, perhaps, being seduced from joining the ancestral ranks.

66 - Adsum. Latin, I am here. Modelled after British public schools, some Sierra Leone schools used Latin in greetings and roll call; e.g., *salve magister*—Greetings, master.

102 - Robben Island. Island prison, South Africa.

108 - al-Mukhlit. Literally: the mixers—i.e., heretics, apostates. The poem opens with extreme rite of ablution.

108 - *Litham.* Face veil.

109 - Masalik al-Jinan. Paths to paradise (after the book by Amadou Bomba).

109 - Abdullah bin Abdul-Muttalib. The prophet Mohammed's father.

110 - Ramadan. Mohammedan season of fasting, an extreme form of which involves not swallowing one's saliva during the hours of fasting.

afterword

■ ■ ■ ■ ■ ■

Lemuel Johnson writes out of the African/Creole experience of
Freetown, Sierra Leone. The name is "portuguese marked in
stones" independent out of England into a third world fed out of
a first world. That's how and where the trouble starts

> Put your money
>
> on zero
> I would bow low, down
> from the waist down
> and so tranquilize the heart, ease
> the warm desire
> to eat human flesh
> the corners of my lips raised
> on zero
>
> on perhaps this or that tedious day
> inheritance is everything
> bones a mere rattle

The white man wove me out of a thousand anecdotes
(Fanon). It is not the consciousness of man that determines his
social being, but his social being that determines his consciousness (Marx). Do not call us *negro*. To call us *negro* is to call us
slave. Call us *prieto* (the Côngolese to a Spanish Capuchin
missionary in the seventeenth century). But that was in another
country. Another time, another place. Africa, integral then, dic-
tated its definitions. The words were words that came in the ships
of Christians —*negro/prieto*. But there was danger to them. Wan-
ton, malicious, they were the bridge that Eshu built with his
penis. The Christian ships came to trade. They traded gold and
slaves. *Oro* was their word for the yellow metal. *Negro* was their
word for slave. The Congolese accepted their word, and attached

to it a social fact they knew, a social being defined by his role.

Somewhere the penis bridge began to break. The Congolese sensed the treacherous word close in a net that bound together biological black skin, cultural black being, with the social being of slave. The bridge broke. The black entered the Western architecture of signs, conjoined as fact and fiction, black slave.

The metamorphosis through the Middle Passage, conjoined master and slave in the enterprise of the Indies. Hawkins, thief, merchant, mariner, sailed to Africa in a seaworthy ship; and got black slaves partly by the sword, partly by trade; he sailed to that other point of the triangle, islands and a continent gotten by storm, with his prey; and there threatened to cut the throat of the Spanish colonists if they did not trade. To traffic in men would call down God's vengeance, Queen Elizabeth had first said. But she profited largely; knighted bold enterprisers right and left. From Virgin Queen the line extends to the "Captain want jig jig" in Freetown, Sierra Leone, recorded by Graham Greene. From here, then, Johnson writes.

Freetown, Sierra Leone is a part of the continent of Africa. Yet, in part, it is also a Creole island, like an island in the Caribbean. The Creole experience is born out of the condition of exile; out of a Middle Passage of body and mind. But if the Caribbean islands were settled as plantations in which the forced labor of the slave was to produce that initial capital that would enable Europe to "take off" into the dynamic paradise of capitalist development, Freetown was to be their exact opposite. For Freetown was to be a monument to that great act of British/European philanthropy—by which the English, having enslaved the Africans for centuries, had accumulated enough wealth from their labor and sale to afford an exquisite frisson of conscience.

The 1772 judgment of Granville Sharp that a black, landed on the soil of Britain was free, was no longer "accepted merchandise" as defined by an earlier English Attorney General, created a group of liberated slaves in England. Freetown was settled by these liberated slaves. Other slaves set free by the British Navy, (recaptured by them from other European nations intent on getting their share of the black loot) were also landed in Freetown. Their Middle Passage was one of departure and return. As Lemuel

Johnson explains it elsewhere

> The city and its people were to be symbols of Christian enlighten-
> ment over the inhumanity of the past. The inhabitants were returned
> "exiled sons of Africa." They had originally come from tribes up and down
> the Slave Coast.
>
> *(The Devil, the Gargoyle and the Buffoon)*

The Cross of Christ was made of wood. The Cross of the
Freetown Christian was an arrangement of genes: black skin, lips,
eyes that existed to negate, perversely, the white skin of Christ.
They took up their Cross and walked. They endured their passion—
"their hell in small places"—and proceeded to sweat in thick
English flannels, to answer in Latin, to endure the incongruity of
their passions, and to re-enact the Crucifixion not as tragedy but
as farce.

"Seek ye first the political Kingdom..." Nkrumah, as prophet, had thought that that was all there was to it. But the political kingdom was his only on hire, lease, so to speak. When he
wouldn't vacate the real owners pulled the strings—and had him
locked out of state and life. And for this and that reason there
will be the devil to pay "out of a ragged root." The alchemist and a
most magical company put money on zero

> but imagine now
> out of an inclination to
> worry the wound, imagine a
> most magical company of young men
> with no address

From here, this country, time and place, Lemuel Johnson
weaves his skein of words. The gods are in exile. In his seven poems
to His Excellency, the poet weaves his verbal skein through a
labyrinth of disparate images, patterning a political motif, a
pattern sketched out of the dust of the new kingdom. He has
confessed to an obsession to transfer to the politics of the second
coming Balzac's indignation: "When at night one sees the beautiful stars here, one just wants to unbutton one's fly and piss on the
heads of all the royal houses." And so the ceremonies of Fort

[131]

Thornton. For purposes of trade, Africa was at first a coast. The coast was dotted with forts. In many of the forts, there was a "factory." Prime Men, Stout Men, Lean Men not sick with the pox were bartered for pieces of cloth, basins, rum, guns, old sheets, beads. The Factory Fort looked out to sea against the other Christian slave-dealing nations. It swivelled around to keep order among the raw material for trade, "a fortress of white stones on a small hill."

Not only a fort, it was a way of life: the very model of the cultural ecology of a white skin; the fairy castle in the imposed enchanted landscape. The Wizard, the Governor himself, castled in white uniform and sun helmet and white feathers, brushed the sky and awed the sun. Here, incarnate, was the accumulated power of a superior juju. All-embracing, a fate that witchdoctors could no longer turn aside; the gods themselves feared so blue an eye. This god commanded the sky.

His spirit moves in Fort Thornton, where he once lived

> an englishman, plumed. in white flannels
> who lived in large houses
> needing more air
> the tropics being, as they are, the tropics

The new Head of State, Caliban in fancy dress, inherits his fort, and his tropics, and his eye. The fort itself was an Ark, its denizen limited. Fearing the flood by fire "we unthatched our houses/in time for rainstorms."

And there are new ceremonies in Fort Thornton after the Second Coming: the Wa-Benzi elite, mannered a la Modigliani, conscious of masks that Picasso, having extracted lines, forms. The woodlocked secret terror, called up and suspended, is made respectable, acceptable, charted points of intellectual chatter up and down flowing stairs: "stationed just so along woodwork and cornice."

Out in the streets the storm beats on the Messianic hope. Nationalism, that magnificent song (Fanon) became mute with the going up of the flag and the military tattoo ushering in the new rulers. The people suck their sorrow, act out the "perverse

[132]

comedy" in "His Excellency: II". They pick their teeth with the sliver of bone left over from The Hope. Disillusion, clear like water:

> this man. *ecce homo*, for love
> of whom some took kerosene lamps
> to the water's edge. the dark edge of water
> and there learned
>
> the sea teaches nothing but water

and the violence against one another, not for an explicit cause but for that simulacrum of action with which briefcase nationalists assure themselves their power exists

> we picked burning kerosene, broke
> skulls with one another
> vagrant calendars in which we saw marks

The end of the journey to the expectation is a return to the same chains:

> the shapes of our skulls are now no different
> than they were. yesterday. the day before yesterday?

In "His Excellency: III" the people attempt to propitiate with traditional bundles of tied red cloth the twisting turns of unpredictable gods; since no man chooses to live in hell.

But the gospels and actions taken by power (even in the first act) gloss the return of hell with words like clouds of dust. Democracy shuffles the cards; takes an absurd delight in forms; its style is all there is to it. The two-party state as definition could not quite fit the Procrustean bed of the neo-colonial whose circumference (their center being outside themselves— London, New York, Washington, Paris, Moscow) needed another name. The Eunuch Scholars, homegrown and foreign, spoke about the One Party State. The Party was His Excellency, the State was His Excellency. His Excellency should live in State.

[133]

Osagyefo this, Osagyefo that, (Armah, *The Beautiful Ones Are Not Yet Born*). And the people? Must make do with statistics; tighten their belts. They are there to be regulated by the State; they *are* by reason of the State. The flag, the anthem, the clapping after names of the powerful are the substances of their soul. They are statistics for the nation's sake:

> ...waiting to forgive
> rulers their odd invasions into the body
> politic our mouths dance
> in shreds in our faces.

But the working out of a little nastiness, the hells in small places, extend in infinite circles; there really are no circles outside this hell. Inferno is multinational. In "His Excellency IV," the Kreen Akrore tribe of Indians hide in rain forests, lurk in fear from the invasion of patient anthropologists, coming with new Christian ships, now secular; not for the sake of their souls, but for science. For the extension of Prospero's magic arts. The Kreen Akrore know enough to fear these men, with power like fireworks in their hands. The anthropologists, wanting to publish another book, to look once more on that which survived, molding its own forms, wait and wait, ready to barter *pacotille* for a way of life.

> and so they wait, these men,
> in supplications of glass bead and axe.

The Pope pronounces *pacem in terris,* long and short words in latin; a violin in Bucharest, a contact lens luxury-pampered dog killed by car in Spain, where Lorca was killed by the "patriotic" forces to preserve nations that were no longer nations—the design that continues the coincidence of untidy passions in time. The design negates itself, disintegrates, reveals the purposeless Fate we are helpless to avert.

In His Excellency V, we have terror, in every-day dress, or dandified at the end of a stick; with a casually elegant holiday in Prague where Power rides in on the gun turrets of Russian tanks. And a student, to protest, provides the local color for the tourist: (hara-kiri with petrol and a match):

the ambitious burning of flesh in a public square

For the poet, a smaller fate. No suicide, since even that has become domestic. Rather than the lamentations of Jeremiah, the picking away at the corner of things; the poet, like poetry, at odds/ with strange emperors. In spite of *pacem in terris,* in correct latin, the peace remained like incense, only sanctifying the genuflexion of the sword. In "His Excellency VII," France, an ancient Christian kingdom, center of Western culture, narcissistic at the sight of its own intellect, echoing to hear the sound of its own language, suffers too that strange disease; sings the Marsellaise; chants a forgotten phrase of a hymn, and erects heroes like ikons. And the nation implies European glory, European destiny; and who dared to hint Marshal Petain did not incarnate the nation rather than the geographically-minded De Gaulle who had finally said Algeria was not biologically French?

These modern grave snatchers, taking Petain out of a 'traitor's grave'—who defines whom?—bury him anew in a Pharoah's tomb of mummified memory. The cinema shows "Wild Strawberries" and coffins with bodies tumble on to the street; fact and fiction conjoined in an apocalypse at noon. We have lost ourselves—our biographies grown to rags—and surrendered these rags to the coffins of our leaders. The proper burial becomes as important as for Antigone. She feared to displease the gods. We fear to lose that rag of a self we have left. Yet *their* First World reburial of fallen leader and fallen self is backed by an expanding growth rate; a standard of living safe behind atomic tests.

Our Excellency, caught in the contradiction between the global expectation and the hunger rising on the horizon, has domesticated obscenity; burial and reburial in the name of the State:

I speak now of death, ours
stumbling as we do upon the white bone of power...

[135]

The labyrinth of white bones encloses a landscape, imposed like a Picasso painting. There is no escape. No breakout. Only the delicate placing of the thread to chart the way that we have come; to explore, like the monk embellishing his text with blue and gold flowers, the corners and angles that spell out new names for hell

> devotions before Mass
> yield us tentative loaves broken
> in Vichy water or water at Lourdes

The post-Independence, neo-colonial agony deprived us of His Excellency as Imperial Devil; and placed instead His Excellency as the Caliban Messiah, who, in the wilderness of jail, agreed to gamble with the devil.

The geographic range of metaphors, Brazil, Bucharest, Prague, a dog run over by car in Spain, a violin in Rumania, the Pope conjuring up peace, encyclically, in Latin, juxtaposes the hells. The cards are dealt out in "an absurd political universe designed by Ionesco."

> we creep among mangrove shrouded creeks
> a supplication of latin things about our necks

Yet—in "Equilibrist"—the protocol for His Excellency must be observed. Legitimacy must not be questioned; a place for everything; everything in its place:

> an itch in the right place/...broken meat back in our bones

* * *

Lemuel Johnson in this first group of poems gives us Caliban Agonistes, blinded by the white bone of instant power, tossed to him when he had once snapped and growled. But the bone had been shaped into dice. The dice were loaded. The obscenity of the neo-colonial experience, worked out in the terrible centuries of Haiti and Latin-America, has spread out

[136]

like a blood-red stain: Christophe of Haiti, whose fact and alienated French Court, complete with dancing master, could not be out done by Cesaire's fiction; then the peculiar terror of an Estrada Cabrera of Guatemala, of a Trujillo, of Duvalier; a particular "underdeveloped terror." As if fear is the only product indigenously produced.

In Part II, the neocolonial event that finally divests Caliban of that which had kept him whole—a dream of revenge against Prospero. But how shall he now revenge himself upon himself? The poet, like the poetry, marks the terror-laden pilgrimage on the *via purgativa.* Cheated of expectation, stripped, we take up our bed, and complaining, begin to crawl.

In Part II, the momentous meeting between Europe and Africa is reduced to its real fact—barter. The poet prefaces "High-life for traders" with Orwell:

> Under the spreading chestnut tree
> I sold you and you sold me.

Out of this barter came Freetown. The land was bought for guns, cloth, rum, glass beads. A history of unequal exchange. And the Creole language formed and fashioned itself out of this barter. Freetown—free trade in cunt priced to suit each dick is fixed by Graham Greene (and others) in its incongruous landscape: the new desert for Western man's wrestling with fine shades of Anglo-Catholic ethics; whilst sellers at the port cry their wares

> Captain want jig jig, my sister pretty girl
> schoolteacher, captain want jig jig

The reductionism of language, the reductionism of a relation; stereotypes confronting one another: exchange value for casual use. Africa, the psychological brother of Europe, its instant pornography. A labyrinth of presuppositions, lurid imaginings, invest Caliban with the Manichean opposite of Europe's conceptual universe.

This second sequence of poems represents, as Johnson

himself explains it, percussive attempts to drum out, drum in, drum together a variety of contradictory experiences which shaped persons of my generation in our exposure to Western culture— Roman Catholicism, Anglican High Church and classical, latinate grammar schools, modelled after Eton and Harrow in England. In one of his best poems—"juju"—we see a verbal landscape, closing down like shutters of ivory filigree on the Freetown port/Fort. The verbal landscape becomes real in a metamorphosis of ecology:

> the bonedust of Sicilian mountains
> growing green with bees and honey and vergil

The title of the poem "Juju," dislocated from its cultural architecture of meaning, becomes a *thing* in the Western definition. *Juju,* meaning a charm dispensed, sold by witchdoctors for either protective or malignant purposes, is separated by a broken bridge from its cosmogony, its theology, its rationale. No longer the expression of the power of man, symbolized in his gods, to confront and master his reality, it is now a charm left over, from the days of power. Its meaning misted, a defensive amulet with which to *suffer* an imposed and alien universe.

Prospero's culture then, is *his* potent counter *juju.* And the European teachers are the witchdoctors of this defense against a too clamorous Freetown reality. For what was then (and is) being fashioned is the black 'humanist' class: new converts to Europe's secular religion of Reason and *humanitas.* Fragments of Greek and Latin, of the iron lays of Beowulf and the sanctified, long-vanished rude vigor of "the Gauls our ancestors." And time—time marked in notches of real enough events in real enough countries; distant, yet close to the inner flesh; close, because conjured up, kept in motion with a juggler's art that imposed consciousness and landscape and affirmed a reality that existed on the pages of *the book.* The true reality of "ideal forms." I read, therefore I am. These pages create me—memories, nostalgia. My life measured out by

> ...an ivory man
> whose hammer marked the terms
> at michaelmas

at trinity
at epiphany but he too believed
in stones an
ivory man of gray ashes...

Witchdoctor, he passed on to me an amulet, a juju, like a
do-it-yourself kit with which to forge cards of identity: signs,
symbols, language, bits of quotes, fragments of allusive references,
clusters of association, sounds and the structuring of sounds with
which to fabricate a biography.

"Juju" juxtaposes existence and consciousness; ambivalent
as to which is which. Consciousness imposed through "words/in
their especial candor"; existence, treacherous, like a dangerous
poem at odds with strange emperors. And so the dialectic of
an existent consciousness and an unconscious, evaded existence:

...madame northway, conjugating
love of st. augustine out of the iron
heat of the equator over our heads,
non amabat, did not love; but then
loving to love, sed amans amare, seeking
querens amare to love beyond our windows...

African St. Augustine; some argue that he was not only North
African but black too. But his cultural world was as far removed
as the jewelled blackness of Sheba ceremonious, on a state visit
to Solomon, is removed from the Freetown students who met
her in the Bible. St. Augustine, seeking to love, did not seek to
exorcise the unreality of a black skin or black gods; he sought
rather to bridge the black Manichean gap that yawned in his
soul. The problematic was different. Here, in "juju", straining
against experience, the poet is conjured into seeking St. Augustine's
tortured seeking to love—while his is another kind of torment:

the smell of black buttocks rubbing raw
faeces on the barks of trees, seeing that paper
was scarce among us, and rags were
needed to keep inquisitions of a too
curious nature from our bones
blackened with lust of st augustine
and carthage burning

[139]

The ambivalence is realized in the metaphors of comparison. The 'witchdoctor': the marvel of that little white english woman, her face a febrile imposition, a charm to be used

> ...against the reign of the beast
> rising out of our empty harbors
> her teeth, small white
>
> so she flicked out conjugations of love
> and drove us mad

In the simulacrum, Eton/Harrow, love, the love of God, intellectualized. Down in the ports, Eros for sale.

For in a sense, the law of price was the law of empire (a delicate shuffling of letters to shape emporio into imperio). And the law too of the superstructure of illusions:

> ...the alphabets of empires met
> outside. in the dry seasons of our windows:
> the tambourines of byzantium
> moist skulls under stone in rome...

obscuring the context:

> ....papers round
> as rosetta stones, and heavier
> between our windows and ourselves.

But the Caliban who revolts uses language to curse. The word is in revolt, the word of Prospero turned against the part of him, his consciousness, that had betrayed him whilst he slept. Caliban hating the creature made of him; yet half-seduced by such Miranda strains.

From imitation he awakes to exorcism, though liberation is only half-imagined, barely glimpsed. "Figures in wood" is a kind of "summary introduction." Implicit here is Ulysses with his ships—the 'patron Saint', ancestral spirit of the West. The ships of Christians descending on the Congolese are here the British Navy which used West African ports during the war. Ulysses, Johnson explains, still comes and still leaves the ports of the One-Eyed in

[140]

some disarray:

> falling out of the sky, foreskins
> peeled back

The poet, using the word in revolt, reverses the images, shuffles the protagonists; the 'villains' are brought full center. The objects of the Western Enterprise become the subjects. Johnson writes:

In a sense, the protagonists of these poems are those like Cyclops, Lazarus ("exorcism"), Shylock ("Shylock, after"), Caliban ("calypso for caliban"), Ophelia ("ophelia at elsinore")—these characters who prowl the fringes of the 'positive humanism' of the imported culture. Perhaps they are more significant to the history and psychology of thirdworlders.

The black cannibals, the mindless hordes, the foils for Tarzan and Jane ("A.T.&P. Ltd.") revolt against the crowd scenes, against the script, factual and verbal. Somewhere in that first encounter, in the trading, the main outlines of the text had been fixed. Caliban revolts against the barter of roles. In the exchange he had lost. How much was still not clear; not even the extent of the occasional gain:

> we bartered, unclear
> what we won or lost...
> ....
> Call us Ishmael, (if you wish) or Barabbas
> or Cain...
>
> the ports lie now in slack water
> our fingers scrape the sides of empty bowls
> and go back to our lips.

In this part, Johnson uses a sequence of long poems in short, tightly rhythmic lines with frequent monosyllabic percussions that provide both hesitation and propulsion for a mixture of sometimes lurching, sometimes dancing outbursts. The basic rhythms, Johnson says, of these acts of exorcism, are derived from

the compulsive drumming of African (or sometimes Caribbean—
"Vèvè" and "Calypso for caliban") rhythms. So the highlife, the
calypso are specifically mentioned. But other beats consciously
followed are voodoo drumbeats ("Vèvè") and the more energetic
form of the highlife, *Goombay,* which survives in creole society
in Sierra Leone. An acrobatic, semi-burlesque, flagrantly erotic
gymnastic of the buttocks, the *goombay* survives in the West
Indies too.

The title of the poem "Vèvè" is taken from the ritual
marks in white made on the floor at the start of voodoo
worship. Voodoo was the syncretistic religion, embracing aspects
of other tribal religions as well as Roman Catholicism, which
provided ideology for the rebellion of the slaves. A religion which
began as subterranean and subversive, it still patterns the life
and the imagination of the vast majority of Haitians. It is also
an affirmation of the gods' migration across the Middle Passage;
their rerooting in the new world. The *vève* marks out the parameters of the ceremony in which the gods, old and new, are summoned to interact in the life of the living.

The poem deals with the invocation for the gate to be
lifted so the gods can enter. The worshipper enclosed in the steps
of the ritual is, like Camus' Sisyphus, whom one must imagine
(for Camus' sanity?) to be happy. *"Il faut imaginer que Sisyphe
est heureux."* But Sisyphus' point of sanity and Camus' may not
coincide, and the worshipper is seen, like Othello, a wheeling
stranger of everywhere. The cosmogony of voodoo is used again
in "covenant." *Baron Samedi,* one of the powerful god-figures,
creator of zombies, is invoked; and a few lines are patterned like
the *vève,* the complex intricate world of meaning, reduced to the
schematic lines of the Haitian 'primitive' painters:

> pick/clear/geometries of repose
> opalescent hieroglyphs
> of bones...

The poem, "witchdoctors," like "juju," seizes on a word,
whose bridge to its original meaning has been broken. The poet,
son of an organist who played on pedal organs ("with their ineffable

quality of hand-barrel-monkey parody and anachronistic sanctity.
I breathed, ate, smelled that sound Sunday after Sunday after
Sunday."), the poet comes into conflict when he enters the imagi-
native world of the witchdoctors. Reduced from the prophets who
could interpret the symbols of a fixed universe of metaphor, when
that universe fell apart they had to take up fragments—jujus—and
convert themselves to technicians:

> disbelieving in the accidental
> we came warily enough
> with raffia brooms
> this other one
> with bamboo whistles, power
> against witchcraft, for/ease of strange sicknesses
> goatskin pouches...

Then came the ships. The witchdoctors come down, skulls
distended, to meet our fates. To others, the ships may have seemed
accidental, a casual event. But they came warily, reading the
signs:

> ...walls that leaned
> in frantic eagerness towards the atlantic

Their doom was in the "gray man," a lover of laterites, a believer
in stones. The creative phase of the neolithic slowly retreats
before this gray "vague man...maddened with granite."

In "a dance of pilgrims" the paradox of Freetown, paradox
of the poet's biography—of his organ-playing father, a provincial
priestly petty bourgeoisie—is well caught, evoked in the first
few lines:

> my father, wheezing aesthete
> before he died...
> ......played
> on pedal organs;
> small-gaited pilgrimages
> peregrinations that
> faded at odd cross roads...

[143]

The modulation of sound that should have echoed in the corners of some gray English provincial town, musty in summer, a decent Hallelujah for Spring, muted in winter, wheezes out here in some arklike transient church against the sound of rain and the silence of drought:

> the two-toned dry
> visitation or wet
> of nature is our inheritance

For the Prodigal in his "canticle," the exile begins in the landscapes: "dutch castles/and/stones/marked in/portuguese." Chronicle, monument and slave trade. The ritual ceremony, the bringing forth of a new child to be presented, *ku omo jade,* is now ambivalent among alien signs. The lions that had seemed formed from the rocks, and caused the Portuguese to give it a name (the Sierra of lions), are seen to be charlatan lions. There is in reality no return; no fatted calf; nor can the "succulent/ passages of/fine women redress the rage/and riot of substance." There is only the awakening to the knowing of himself, native now only to exile:

> and I come to myself/drumming/
> a canticle of dry/sticks
> traveling

"Calypso for Caliban," which is central to the title, begins with the awakening to the reality of his inheritance. The island now returned to him is a chain of leached bones. Prospero has joined the ancestral gods—Papa Prospero, Papa Legba. But he introduces into the licensed ritual disorder that is a part of the Voodoo ceremony a dualism that moves in the coordinates of medieval bestiary: the Beast is to be born white. The dialect of the Calypso form takes on the wasteland of the western sexual psyche; the "vaginas" are "derelict"; and the Immaculate Conception satirized, negated:

> him goin to kiss the whores
> in she certain parts...

[144]

The calypso form, the Creole dialect, its assumptions free from the sexual *angst* of Prospero's kingdom, play with the "beast" role assigned to Caliban. But Caliban, poet, educated and therefore "partaking of the same collective unconscious as the European" (Fanon) can afford no such ironic distance. The geography of his imagination has been charted from Homer's Ulysses to Eliot's "what seas what shores what gray rocks and what islands." He has identified with the pilots of these psychic journeys from Homer to Tarzan ("A.T.&P. Ltd."). It is the world of Voodoo and Calypso to which he is alien; to which he must make a conscious return. His unconscious, patterned by the menace of our education, negates the fact of his being black, of being Caliban, Polyphemus blinded:

> the stake/in the center of my head...
> believing nothing but/the black/water
> (once my eye)
>
> but they go
> the sun visible
> and
> penelope waiting
> *("Exorcism")*

To negate the negation the poet can only choose its anti-symbols, defined by itself. Making these anti-symbols his, accepting their fact and fiction. It is a complicated psychic maneuver. He pays for this schizophrenic consciousness—only through Ulysses can he reach Cyclops; only through Prospero reach Caliban—with new areas of pain explored, grayer rocks, more sunless seas, more Circeian islands. Through the Virgin Mary, in "calypso for caliban," he sees the beast. The Beast is himself.

> the Virgin Mary/keep the carnival of lent
> the feast of ashes/in the dance/of the open thigh
>
> the flexed knee while/
>
> black beasts

```
prowl
the pastures of my brain.
```

Through Miranda he sees his own face in the mirror:

```
derelict/I prowl/these quays
dissatisfied with my face
prospero
against the face of your daughter...

I grow dissatisfied
with this and that corner of my face.
```

In "highlife for traders" the Creole dialect and the Creole form exist in a precarious mockery of itself. The items traded are pitiful in their precision. The irony lies in the enormity of their historical significance. In the *Autobiography of a Runaway Slave,* the old Cuban, Montejo, tells us that it was the African's love of the color scarlet that had trapped them into slavery. When the sea peddlers waved scarlet handkerchiefs in the hot and oleous air, we ran down to the Christian slave traders' ships, bartered our future for a piece of scarlet cloth:

```
item: 2 bags lead
balls
10 yards of
scarlet
scarlet
cloth
item: for a stout man

item: for a lean man
not sick
with the pox.
```

And the barter continues. The new leaders, "their excellencies," make the same unequal exchange. They root like hogs among the luxuries of power, the nation-state becoming consumer product:

the politics of the second coming/thinking it was chopful

[146]

The people in Achebe's *Man of the People* pointed out that since the colonizers enriched themselves, had eaten, why not the new leaders? Let them all eat as long as they ate within limits; didn't eat enough for the owner to see. But once there had been an owner—in a context that forced the tribal gods to enforce limits on those who would tend to eat too greedily, that is, to chop. Now that context had gone and with it the gods. Some eat gold protein, others starve on starch. The feasting of the greedy is noisy and ostentatious—even flamboyantly indelicate. Hence the Creole is the precise instrument of communication:

> I chop/you chop/we all chop
> and, oga,
> palaver finish
> in the kingdom

"Exorcism" and "shylock, after" move within the parameters that are the poet's strength—and so avoid the tendency in the occasional poem toward verbal indulgence: a too verbal agony. The poet has told of his schooling and what he refers to as the seductive Latin phrases of our exposure to Roman Catholicism. "Exorcism" is dedicated to his teacher (English?). The poem is formal, a space marked out by cadences and a sense of procession, penitential. He exorcises the place built for them, storied, by strangers, narrow as a calvinist's ark. Yet, when there is a death in the house, in this same place, all mirrors and pictures are turned to the wall. This gesture is part of the ritual of African religions, which survived the seas into the Caribbean; and back to Sierra Leone. The spirit of the deceased, due to be released through ritual into the clear status of ancestor, must see no reflection of himself that could trick him to stay, trap him in the dimension of the present.

So many fragments in "exorcism"—from what seas, what gray shores, what rocks, what islands, arklike surviving of floods! The poet creates his essence from such rags of memory: Titian-eyed ladies, madrigals, Chaucer, candid in language, announcing Spring; then the Cyclops blinded in his cave, like a great yawn in the earth, impotent, hearing Ulysses just out of reach.

[147]

<pre>
          the ships
          too far
          the rocks
          too heavy
</pre>

And then Lazarus, resentful of exile from death, of being the proof of Jesus' miracle, cursed with life

<pre>
          set upon
          by wishes not my own
</pre>

Called by the *magister* Jesus, Lazarus must respond, take up his life like an alien bed, on new and alien terms. Once more reduced to apprenticeship; to be molded by the master's skill. (Some West African schools are so "gentlemanly latinate"—as Johnson tells us—that roll calls are done in Latin:

<pre>
          Salve Magister greetings, master
          Salvete pueri   greetings, boys
</pre>

And so, in the poem, Lazarus answers *adsum,* I am here.

Lazarus comes reluctantly out of the dark back into the painful light of Jesus. Shylock, assaulted in the ghetto of his Jewish being, is dragged into an alien universe, the scapegoat for its self condemnation; to find himself cramped against the night, condemned, against his will baptized, aroused to Christian life, his true self being able to survive only by the direst cunning:

<pre>
          in nomine/by name the jew/sed semper/the jew/
          golem in yellow/gold pax tecum
</pre>

Caliban/poet goes on his travels. There are no further seas for him. His journey is psychic, testing this fabricated self, as Quixote his helmet, through his responses to the world that had sent out its myth to make him. Thus, there is a group of poems in which the responses to places are more immediate, "less enchanted into mythology." They record, some more piercing than others, the bruise on the heart that these responses bring.

[148]

The cities are haunted by sickness; the interior walled with the disgust of the flesh, women in particular. The city receives the viaticum, the sacrament of the eucharist given to those in mortal danger

> here in the center, the acid
> perfumes of badly douched women who
> sit crosslegged at cocktails...
> ....
> these things leave a bruise in the heart

Outside, the cold cracks like a whip/wild geese feint paths over the edge of the sky/and fly south. Even further removed, on the journey back, from the plane

> the continent surprises; brown earth
> edging the smooth tips of the southern atlantic
> *("Viaticum")*

Then there are the varied textured encounters, through the European Grand Tour, taking in places and women—finding carnal closeness, that is distant:

> a syntax of yellow barricades
> hangs between your speech and mine

And the Tour takes in the coincidences of "hell in small places": soviet jews in soviet prisons ("viaticum"); soviet jews cheated in Israel's heaven where eggs didn't lay about the streets as believed ("san rafael"). Pan becomes another guise for Caliban through whom conception would come again to Bethlehem but "for no real purpose." Then varied responses to women, real and imagined, exorcising the ghost of Miranda; but here is no brave world; more preferable, Cleopatra's mummy, fabled with reality ("coronation"). In Venice, romantic with gondolas, the Venetian gentlemen sing no serenades under the moon. Rather they are busy...

> ...wondering how/well you (blonde of hair)
> and I did it.

[149]

Venice, locus of Othello—fishbones, screams of urgent cats, water that sucks at the rotting stones of hotels ("Venice"). The poet and the Grand Tour respond to, circle Caliban's priapic image: the ultimate phallus yet though "the waters are warm/ between the corners of your blue white legs/there are bones in my private parts...

"Letter to my tailor" narrows down to the bonehard, enclosed predicament of the self, taken to walking with care. The world is mined

> the human mind, it's true, survives
> all but its own hanging
> lately, I have taken to walking
> with my elbows close to my body...

Twelve stitches inside the mouth, should keep the word in place and elbows keep the rebellion of brittle bones polite.

Part Five moves into a different mood—the poet responding to the poetic ecology of Northern Nigeria. Lemuel Johnson was born there, of Sierra Leone parents, and it lives in imagination as "a sometimes perplexing configuration in my childhood memories of sand, river confluences, camels, the Koran and parched, walled cities." These poems open a mood of fan-like delicacy. The landscape is not the verbal, literary landscape of earlier poems. Here the poet recreates an ecology that is not strained through the tension of a conflictual situation. Water flows through these poems, crystal water on which float precise bamboo-ribbed sails, the water of the rite of ablution, of purification with which the Al-mukhlit poem opens. But this is no psychic purgation, rather a translucent age-old pattern, too patterned for the torment or terror of the Christian psyche.

These poems, technically too, have the clarity of water: "having shaved the insides of/our nostrils and ears sit down to food for which/there exists no botanical names." There is contrast between an opalescent relation of river and architecture:

the upper reaches of the river curve away/

[150]

> from long-jointed minarets
> the scales of fresh water fish are in our clean nostrils

and the stagnant damming up of poverty, traditional, unhallowed. Djenne smells like a drowned lake and there are dead fishes among the roots of bamboo trees/the red eyes of hungry lepers search among broken pots.

Here in a backwater where there are no deltas, no commercial activity of profit to the West (as in the south). Time and Nature are repetitive, in fixed monotony like prayer chants:

> in december the harmattan blows cold sand
> our gray fingers keep warm inside the gray bellies of fish
> there are small scales floating to the deltas
> on the thin entrails of the dead

Here the question of black and white is absent. Black skin is one more feature of life and its ecology. And black skin, gray with cold, and accustomed hunger, writes a hieroglyph enclosed in its own meaning. The tone of this poem is continued in "split fences." Prospero's economic system is distant. It may have helped to reinforce the cycle of waiting, the limited hope but its effects are silent. Prospero is absent. His culture is ineffectual against these minarets of consciousness, this universe summoned into being by the muezzin's call. Prospero's arrogance, laughable in the face of a Nature, of an earth that turns the wrong way, where rivers wash the veins out of dry mountains. Here Prospero's linear time has no meaning; and seems as alien as his progress. Here numbers, squares recur in a kind of dry and rigid mathematics. The limits are known, fixed. There is the calm of bitter certitude.

> our expectations are modest;
> we search the verses of the dead son of Abdullah bin Abdul
> > Muttalib
> we pick at sores, they heal
> there is silence between our teeth

The task, the pattern, like the river washing the veins from the mountains, reweaves itself, the same texture, the same skein.

But there are intrusions, insidious. In the poem "Immigrants" I wheel discarded british bicycles. The technological fact is an accepted excrescence of a nature which has become poverty-stricken; an extended shanty town of discarded hoops, tins, tires. Here flies mate on the dried spit; there is the smell of burning flesh/half-finished faces. Man survives only by gestures of defense plucked, like rags, from the old patterns

> we ululate and keep dogs away from those we burn.
> there is no wind.

But in this shanty town space of huddled, temporary Nature, there are areas still of silent water for "ablution." There is stillness, opening like a fan: the ceased flick of washerwomen's paddles.

> I will tether the canoe to a river willow
> the river is full
> crested cranes fly banking against the moon
> shadows remain on the paddles of washerwomen.

The sound patterns of the poem emerge from a new ecology; the literary landscape and the sound of the Sicilian bees, buzzing in Vergilian landscape exist only as absence. Here we have an old landscape, new storied; named and existent; a landscape of sound and silence.

* * *

One returns in Part VI to a harsher response. No childhood memories here smelling of faeces, or shimmering with sunlit sails; but the confrontation, the response to the new imperial center: the emporium that has done away with the Vergilian myth of Empire. Not now to *regere populos,* to teach black boys to scan Vergil, struggle with *querens amare* of St. Augustine amidst tin roofs and temporary structures. Rather to educate them to become consumers; to integrate their souls with Coca Cola and Cadillacs.

The poet makes a *rite de passage* from Vergil, St. Augustine, the conjugation of love and bark-raw buttocks, to a new reality, one out to:

> ...wreck the delicate
> phrases of our british tutelage

The visa is the initiation seal into *Playboy* models of men. The black obsessed with his own reality, cuts out his cardboard outline in sharp clothes:

> narrow lapels and narrow-brimmed hats
> slanted
> dangling in dance like empty clothes
> on meat hooks

The hysteria rises, held on a tight rein, once one comes to terms with the absurd fantasy of trapped skyscrapers, dealing with it by small defenses; learning the way its technology works; behaving correctly, as if nothing:

> down in the hotel's toilet
> my children and I urinate with ease
> for ten cents against white porcelain
> We get enough paper/to keep pissdrops from
> the flaps of our trousers/my daughter's
> knickers...

In Freetown, there had never been enough. Now here, where toilet paper is a multi-million dollar industry, there is infinite choice, so many colors, so many patterns. The small breasts of his wife are untaxed. So far, so good. Then the break-up begins; the surrealist nightmare cannot be held at bay by the ritual of small actions. Hell is domestic here:

> ...my color falls apart in my hands
> ....
> in new york city I
> await flight patterns hanging
> in new york city by
> fingertips to my skin.

But Caliban can dress himself in Prospero's hair. Here fabricated, ready-made men are for sale. In "shopping list," he can buy, by mail:

> ...new hair
> that is smoothslick gold
> like fish streaking for deep waters
> at the edge of the mediterranean

The hair divides. Matthew, the little boy, wants to play neighbors with my children; he stares through the glass but his hair is the wrong color. Color, between the eyes outside the glass, and the eyes inside, is taut, like a high tension wire. The tower of Babel—of tongues; and multi-colored hair.

Tension strains, twists in on itself, agony without release in "Feb 14th & the bed of the king of France." Violence, not now like cherry pie, but casual, anonymous, like a mass production line; fragments of images leaning on paper-littered streets; and fungoid men against walls, high on life and screams of jangled wires. Violence seeps around the angles and corners of the streets:

> the shards of broken heads
> tonight are jazzily easily
> cacophonous tonight three
> black men/under stress/have/
>
> been shot, in proportion, by
> three policemen,
>   under stress.....
> and impolite bullets under stress
> in the ears of undertakers.....

Through this and the following poems the poet works out and over to the far side of despair. The poems become patterned, integral again in "Children's choice." Experience can have form; no longer need broken images be huddled together, like a pack of cards crazily dealt out by the joker, dealing himself first and last of all. Death enters in "Children's choice" and reasserts old significances in the neon wilderness:

may you keep to yourself
even the delicate cartilage of your nose
against the work of maggots
and the weight of stones

The protocol of death, in the next poem, exorcises the terror of unshriven exit, in a world of reverence. Death is no longer the affirmation of one's existence (once invested by the gods); it is now deserted by them, reduced to its biological negation:

Old women limp beyond me
coughing up their livers in small pieces
on frozen plains

the deranged underwears of changing
old men change merely to plug
the leakages of private griefs

let them...

I die keeping the cancers away
from the rattling of my voice.

In the last poem, we return to the wrestling with literary 'angels'. Johnson has explained:

I suspect I'm interested in Judas, Ophelia, Shylock for the same reasons, thirdworlders all of them; outsiders, but not heroic ones like Manfred or Childe Harold, rather, confused, impotent, schizophrenic—which, I suppose, is the way I see my problems with Prospero's apparently inexplicable prosperity in the light of our (my?) inexplicable dispossession. (Also Quasimodo's.)

"Quasimodo's bolero" moves within the fields of force of drum and bell; Quasimodo twice-disinherited, as deformed outsider; as black companion to bell and gargoyles, crucified on a belfry of signs; in an iron lay that defined its heroes: and denied its villains with:

...the fat of metal
that shivers in shocks of ecstasy
through the open spaces
of my rags...

The bell's resonance, the beat of its tongue against iron and bronze and the gargoyle desperation of Quasimodo/Caliban ringing in salvation for another—to affirm the negation of himself! Quasimodo, now questioning his fief to the Western world, grown cynical; sour like Caliban, strips off melodramatic evasion of sentiment:

> my sometime six-inch penis leaks
> stale water below my legs
> and the bottoms of my feet fly
> over the flagstones there are black fields
> below black with faeces with
> the stale faeces...

The bells are a magnificat of terror and anguish, haunted by the cough of drums. Caliban's Bethlehem is come round at last under a doom-laden star. The shepherds watch Mannix on T.V. The Wise Men have gone about their petroleum and gold investments in Africa. Judas/Caliban/Shylock/Polyphemus/Lazarus/Quasimodo is set free from the white shadow of the Cross. The countryside invades the cities of the earth. Cyclops in iron ships bear upon Ithaca. Caliban hammers out magic towers of mythology, to imprison Sicilian mountains, green with bees, honey and Vergil. He imposes his landscape now, existential, like the horn of Armstrong, mocking his own pretense of lyric cadences for an agony as dry as bone, causal as water, matter of fact.

Out of this agony-as-farce, Caliban announces his Annunciation with brazen images, upon the world:

> my back swells with the noise of breaking wind
> and the urgency of bronze and iron
> copper and iron giving birth
> to a dance of concave bones.

Sylvia Wynter
Jamaica, W. I.